Lew Welch's Books

Lew Welch

SELECTED POEMS

Preface by Gary Snyder
Edited by Donald Allen

Grey Fox Press
Bolinas · California

First printing March 1976.

Library of Congress Cataloging in Publication Data

Welch, Lew.
    Selected poems.

    Includes index.
    PS3573.E45A6   1976   818'.5'408   75-44269
    ISBN 0-912516-20-8

Grey Fox Press books are distributed by Book People, 2940 Seventh Street, Berkeley, California 94710.

What we recognize as poetry, different from rock lyrics say, carries a large body of cultural and archetypal lore ("makings") in loops from the past, also aiming into the future. The poems in *Ring of Bone* have an underlying drone-tone, like the tamboura of Indian music: a rich, basic oriental and occidental humane poetic tradition.

Lew Welch writes lyrical poems of clarity, humor, and dark probings. The poems brought together in this selection are the major works of a man who of his forty-five years of life in the west gave twenty-one to poetry. His work stands in the context of San Francisco poetry renaissance: the post-World War II libertarian energy of striving to further develop the possibilities of open-form poetry. The heart of the book is the "Hermit Poems" and "Way Back" sections—poems evoking, covering, the time spent in retreat and practice at a cabin in the mountains of coast north California deep up rivers, still Yurok land. In those works Lew really achieved the meeting of an ancient Asian sage-tradition, the "shack simple" post-frontier back country out-of-work workingman's style, and the rebel modernism of art. He returned to the Bay Area at the inception of the over-heavy flowering of hippie culture. It is instructive how these poems have the essence but cut through the psychedelic baroque.

As for poetics, jazz musical phrasing of American speech is one of Lew Welch's clearest contributions. First taught to write in natural speech and in terms of the musical phrase by Williams and Pound, he turns sometimes to street-talk, street-jive, blues, bop rhythms; and can score it on the page. This is done without cuteness or obscurity. Indeed, all these poems have *music* and *clarity* of language, and a compression such that "the words stop, but the meaning keeps going on." His reading of Chinese poetry and Japanese haiku in translation sharpened eye and ear, but led to imitation only when in fun.

Behind, and informing, the playfulness and skill of these poems, is the evolving wisdom of a man who was on the Way. Over the years the practice becomes more and more Taoist-Buddhist; Chinese poet-sage image wryly turned. More sardonically, the Red Monk as Zen jikijitsu commentator speaks with strict compassion to the glamorous Leo in all of us. Ultimately Lew's poems are devotional songs to the Goddess Gaia: Planet Earth Biosphere: and he is truly one of the few who have Gone Beyond, in grasping the beauty of that ecstatic Mutual Offering called the Food Chain.

Lew and I were brothers and fellow-workers from early. Poets are the sons of witches; understanding the tradition of Muses is contingent on that. Living with the image of the Teeth Mother was the darker side of Lew's songs. He drank far too much, had a way with guns, and took one with him into the woods, never to be seen again, in May of 1971. This is predicted in one of his last pieces, "Song of the Turkey Buzzard." Lew clearly overleaped one more time, and accomplished his own death in his own way: his body has never been found. In "Courses" Lew says,

> Guard the Mysteries!
> Constantly reveal Them!

Mystery: the life of poetry (though poets are always complaining) is without equal. There is nothing to regret.

Gary Snyder

Contents

THIS BOOK IS FOR MAGDA

•

What strange pleasure do they get who'd

wipe whole worlds out,

ANYTHING,
to end our lives, our

wild idleness?

But we have charms against their rage—
must go on saying, "Look,
if nobody tried to live this way,
all the work of the world would be in vain."

And now and then a son, a daughter, hears it.

Now and then a son, a daughter

gets away

•

CHICAGO POEM

I lived here nearly 5 years before I could
    meet the middle western day with anything approaching
Dignity. It's a place that lets you
    understand why the Bible is the way it is:
Proud people cannot live here.

The land's too flat. Ugly sullen and big it
    pounds men down past humbleness. They
Stoop at 35 possibly cringing from the heavy and
    terrible sky. In country like this there
Can be no God but Jahweh.

In the mills and refineries of its south side Chicago
    passes its natural gas in flames
Bouncing like bunsens from stacks a hundred feet high.
    The stench stabs at your eyeballs.
The whole sky green and yellow backdrop for the skeleton
    steel of a bombed-out town.

Remember the movies in grammar school? The goggled men
    doing strong things in
Showers of steel-spark? The dark screen cracking light
    and the furnace door opening with a
Blast of orange like a sunset? Or an orange?

It was photographed by a fairy, thrilled as a girl, or
    a Nazi who wished there were people
Behind that door (hence the remote beauty), but Sievers,
    whose old man spent most of his life in there,
Remembers a "nigger in a red T-shirt pissing into the
    black sand."

It was 5 years until I could afford to recognize the ferocity.
    Friends helped me. Then I put some
Love into my house. Finally I found some quiet lakes
    and a farm where they let me shoot pheasant.

Standing in the boat one night I watched the lake go absolutely
    flat. Smaller than raindrops, and only
Here and there, the feeding rings of fish were visible 100 yards
    away — and the Blue Gill caught that afternoon
Lifted from its northern lake like a tropical! Jewel at its ear
    Belly gold so bright you'd swear he had a
Light in there. His color faded with his life. A small
    green fish . . .

All things considered, it's a gentle and undemanding
    planet, even here. Far gentler
Here than any of a dozen other places. The trouble is
    always and only with what we build on top of it.

There's nobody else to blame. You can't fix it and you
    can't make it go away. It does no good appealing
To some ill-invented Thunderer
    Brooding above some unimaginable crag . . .

It's ours. Right down to the last small hinge it
    all depends for its existence
Only and utterly upon our sufferance.

Driving back I saw Chicago rising in its gases and I
    knew again that never will the
Man be made to stand against this pitiless, unparalleled
    monstrocity. It
Snuffles on the beach of its Great Lake like a
    blind, red, rhinoceros.
It's already running us down.

You can't fix it. You can't make it go away.
    I don't know what you're going to do about it,
But I know what I'm going to do about it. I'm just
    going to walk away from it. Maybe
A small part of it will die if I'm not around

    feeding it anymore.

A ROUND OF ENGLISH

for Philip Whalen

1.
The day I first woke up everybody had scabs on their eyes
and I couldn't get to a mirror fast enough.

Everybody said that nothing had changed 'cause nothing ever could.

I thought I knew how to talk, but somebody showed up who
could have heard it all, and I didn't have a thing to say.

Somebody else said, "Proust."

2.
It was all about a lady who gave vulgar soirees.
It was all about whales, and a harpoon sharp enough to shave with.
And "Look,
if you're really interested,
which I seriously begin to doubt,
you'll get it from the guys he stole it from."

She barêd her bosom
I whupped out m'knife
Carved my initials on her thin breast bone

"Thin brass dome, beautiful!
How'd you ever think of a thin brass dome?"

7

And somebody young as we were sagged into the room,
face all caked with blood and
clothes still damp with the natural leakage of a
5-day wine drunk:

> *"Well, I may be inverted,*
> *but thank God I'm not insatiable."*

There'll be BEANS BEANS BEANS enough for you and me
in the STORE
in the STORE

(Fry - HEIT)

3.

I always used a certain kind of notebook because it took the
ink well.

"Saints are well fish"

> *Iridescent as horse fly*
> *Ink should be*
> *Should float upon the*
> *Agéd scroll*

And lost my rained-on *Swann's Way*, notes on the flyleaf,
"Water-lily Image," "His old Church." Lost
my footlocker full of notes
letters from cracking-up friends
hall notes from landlords
impassioned scribblings from urinal walls
carbons of letters (my own so young)

> *Please don't leave garbage in the
> hallway as garbage attracts termites
> and termites are the one thing we
> haven't had*

4.
After the Taozers and Hindoos and Parables of Zen,
the Writers by Century and all of their friends,
who knows how many sick Frenchmen and
all those 'Murcans comin' on free,
I never had time to read.

> *Came then to Chicago, to
> matriculate
> among the pro's.*

●

I always expected to find, among those buttresses,
some rude Falstaffian man, surrounded by dogs,
polishing at the armour of his lord . . .
heard, instead, the voices of children, raised in song:

Shakespeare Milton
Shakespeare Milton

Shelley as well
Shelley as well

Sarah something Teasdale
Sarah something Teasdale

Edith M. Bell
Edith M. Bell

5.
I wonder what I thought I'd find in all those books —
probably what's there from time to time, but
how could I have known that?

I wonder what it looked like then.

Some young horrifying thing all
muddy, and lurching, and
proud?

I sat brooding where the park is Japanese
with slanting rock and undernourished trees:

> Is beauty that's blown from the oldest Sea
> But beauty that's borne in the Mind's Eye? We
> Who treasure it, just vain deluded men?
>
> *Pourquoi voulez-vous donc qu'il m'en souvienne*

Taut hams
    shove her skirt
now to the right
    now to the left

There is nothing more to do today
nothing more to do

Nothing more to do today
nothing more to do

today
to do today

And no explanation but the oldest one of all:

    Lady, your visit alone is important to me
    though I'm often inadequate to your simple demand.

    For your sake I am unemployable in the world of Man,
    am often cruel to friends, and
    cannot keep my promises.

    Just when I think I know you, you take capricious form:
    chair to sea to rock to littlegirl reading on the
    supermarket steps; tongue between teeth, so
    serious!
    legs spread wide (a characteristic pose)

    O Waitress in a soiled uniform,
    finally bringing me my check

    "And will that be all sir?"

        Yes.

MEMO SATORI

*There will be a policy meeting of key staff personnel in
Mr. Trout's office at 9 A.M., Monday. Please attend.*

Well, here we go to bother out of all proportion:

    1) The scarcely bargain and a somewhat gain.
    2) The bought, unknown, incompetent.
    3) The might be someday done

2½ hours ago a bell rang
> *I live a winter morning,*
> *half-clothed in a dark room,*
> *trying to plan the day*

Drove through 16 miles of snow, slick roads, 35,000 speeding cars
& didn't kill a soul, or even
skid
> *The radiator lulls me now, my*
> *shoes begin to steam and dry*

              *   *   *   *   *

It happens, or can, almost anywhere, but here.
The sparrow at the Zoo:

        blurry little bird in his bath of dust
        just inside the Camel's cage

dances off the pines and waves of a small Wisconsin Lake,
flickers on attention we can't quite hold still, till

        WHOP,   a

perfect clarity in
stopped time, and I

almost drove the boat against the swimmer's dock & drowned!

        never use a motor, man,

you gotta row
to go!

I FLY TO LOS ANGELES

Way down

In 1952 Chicago 10 above 0 in my gabardine raincoat handed
down to me by Dan Drew, too small, waiting in snow for a bus

I saw the silver glint of 4 motor airplane far up the sky, in the
clear cold and getting colder sun, the sunned-on snow drift
pink and floating violet against my tearing eyeballs and

Why? Why me way down here, all the rest flying, packed away
in too expensive airplanes, off, off to the whole world sliding
down mountains on little sticks, with bright-banded Norway
sweaters and 10 dollar sunglasses on?

Why me in Chicago Christmas Post Office 9.90 a day ain't got
no place to go in my gabardine coat?

So I caught pneumonia forgot to get my refund on the income
tax quit school got psychoanalyzed and

I've been buying warmer and warmer overcoats ever since.

I'm in those airplanes all the time now at Company Expense,
the finest in the air, free drinks pamperings airtravel cards and
right on schedule at the very best time of the day

While California my home sits quietly way on down there—
river stuffing his mud in the surf's mouth and a funny green
scum crawling between the folded mountains. I couldn't figure
it out, we'd had floods in California.

But I'm too crazy for this. It came too late or wrong or maybe
it costs too much that isn't money. Anyway people even the
squarest are starting to worry about me all the time and I get
more and more ashamed and tired.

TAXI SUITE

1. AFTER ANACREON

When I drive cab
    I am moved by strange whistles and wear a hat.

When I drive cab
    I am the hunter. My prey leaps out from where it
    hid, beguiling me with gestures.

When I drive cab
    all may command me, yet I am in command of all who do.

When I drive cab
    I am guided by voices descending from the naked air.

When I drive cab
    A revelation of movement comes to me. They wake now.
    Now they want to work or look around. Now they want
    drunkenness and heavy food. Now they contrive to love.

When I drive cab
    I bring the sailor home from the sea. In the back of
    my car he fingers the pelt of his maiden.

When I drive cab
    I watch for stragglers in the urban order of things.

When I drive cab
    I end the only lit and waitful thing in miles of
    darkened houses.

2. PASSENGER POEM, THE NURSE

I don't like cats kittens are all right I guess
you can love 'em when they're little, like people,
but then they grow up and take advantage of you

and how can you love 'em anymore?

3. PASSENGER POEM, MRS. ANGUS

There's lots of death down there
and a fish the Spanish people eat
couldn't get me near one
red they are, like meat
Bonita.

A famous jockey and two other lads,
and him with a big race comin' up Sunday,
went out at night in a little boat
and they was washed I think
to a place of reptiles, and eaten, for
none of 'em was ever found.

Yon place scares me.

4. PASSENGER POEM, THE MAILMAN

"I understand you had a parade today," I said,
flipping the meter over and driving into traffic.
Without so much as a yes he got right into it
(carefully, with many pauses):

> *We wore*
> *regulation letter-carrier's*
> *uniforms,*
> *except for the leggin's*
> *of course,*
> *and the*
> *helmets. Whatdayacallem?*

"You mean the kind of hat Teddy Roosevelt wore when
he went to Africa to shoot lions, Pith Helmets?"

> *That's right*
> *helmets.*

> *Fellow next to me carried*
> *the association banner.*

> *I carried*
> *the American Flag.*

> *It looked real*
> *nice.*

5. TOP OF THE MARK

for John Wieners

I guess it's only natural that they
go about their planet as they do
all night long:

> Top of the Mark, St. Francis,
> Fairmont, Sir Francis Drake

What a price they pay for what they see!

> *I cannot help them*
> *I will not cheat them*

Yesterday I drove the actual Cab of Heaven . I am
    Leo . I was born this way

> my mane is longer than the sun

APOTHEOSIS OF LEO

Digesting a succulent Gazelle,
"Yum Yum," said Leo
and turned into a giant round rock.

The rock said,

"It's cold out here. I think I'll
spin around that Star

for a couple of Kalpas."

And Leo laughed, for he was the Sun,

and said,

"Yum Yum"

IN ANSWER TO A QUESTION FROM P. W.

In Mexico I'll finish the novel I'll write, rough, while
    fire-watching in Oregon.
The problem is, what kind of typewriter to pack in?

I ought to be able to live 6 months in Mexico on what I
    earn on the Mountain in 4.
They say you can buy dirty books down there.

Since they give you horses to pack things in, how would it
    be if I took in a big old typewriter and left it there?
They don't give you horses to pack things out.

Going to Mexico by motorcycle would be the coolest, but
    Thoreau warns against any undertaking that
    requires new clothes.
Walking is pure, but I haven't achieved simplicity yet.
I'll never willingly hitchhike again.

Next winter I can buy Snyder's Austin for $200, but how
    can I get the money together?
They repossessed my Oldsmobile.
I've never made the foreign-country scene.

Like the sign over the urinal: "You hold your future
    in your hand."
Or what the giant black whore once said, in the back of my cab:

> *"Man, you sure do love diggin' at my*
> *titties, now stop that. We get where*
> *we going you can milk me like a*
> *Holstein, but I gotta see your*
> *money first."*

3.
Mile-high humps of granite are like bubbles in our
          Cream-of-Wheat
hundred-foot trees like tiny moss on mile-high
          humps of Cream-of-Wheat
Inverted Ant Lion traps, quivering?
On top?

An interesting play of the mind, but only
an interesting play of the mind:
The scales are off my eyes . . .

I saw humanity merge into one last giant
junky, waiting (for The Man), on some last
barren ridge, last,
most horrible vision of Man-Hooked Man . . .

Or make it gentler. Nail a sign to one of these trees.

          VOTE HERE

for example

4.
after dinner I took a walk
and She said so sweetly
(finally finding me alone)

          Why do men look for lost cities
          when lost groves grow
          just over the next knoll and the
          next, and next . . .

And all that has always sickened me,
all I know my kind will always be,
dropped away again
into the same old poem

          you bear with me.

WOBBLY ROCK

for Gary Snyder

"I think I'll be the Buddha of this place"

*and sat himself
down*

1.
It's a real rock

(believe this first)

Resting on actual sand at the surf's edge:
Muir Beach, California

(like everything else I have
somebody showed it to me and I found it by myself)

Hard common stone
Size of the largest haystack
It moves when hit by waves
Actually shudders

(even a good gust of wind will do it
if you sit real still and keep your mouth shut)

Notched to certain center it
Yields and then comes back to it:

Wobbly tons

2.
Sitting here you look below to other rocks
Precisely placed as rocks of Ryoanji:
Foam like swept stones

(the mind getting it all confused again:
"snow like frosting on a cake"
"rose so beautiful it don't look real")

Isn't there a clear example here—
Stone garden shown to me by
Berkeley painter I never met
A thousand books and somebody else's boatride ROCKS

(garden)

EYE

(nearly empty despite this clutter-image all
the opposites cancelling out a
CIRCULAR process: *Frosting-snow*)

Or think of the monks who made it 4 hundred 50 years ago
Lugged the boulders from the sea
Swept to foam original gravelstone from sea

(first saw it, even then, when finally they
all looked up the
instant AFTER it was made)

And now all rocks are different and
All the spaces in between

(which includes about everything)

The instant
After it is made

3.

I have been in many shapes before I attained congenial form
All those years on the beach, lifetimes . . .

When I was a boy I used to watch the Pelican:
It always seemed his wings broke
And he dropped, like scissors, in the sea . . .
Night fire flicking the shale cliff
Balls tight as a cat after the cold swim
Her young snatch sandy . . .

> *I have travelled*
> *I have made a circuit*
> *I have lived in 14 cities*
> *I have been a word in a book*
> *I have been a book originally*

Dychymig Dychymig: (riddle me a riddle)

> Waves and the sea. If you
> take away the sea

Tell me what it is

4.

Yesterday the weather was nice there were lots of people
Today it rains, the only other figure is far up the beach

> (by the curve of his body I know he leans against the
> tug of his fishingline: there is no separation)

Yesterday they gathered and broke gathered and broke like
Feeding swallows dipped down to pick up something ran back to
Show it
And a young girl with jeans rolled to mid-thigh ran
Splashing in the rain creek

> *"They're all so damned happy—*
> *why can't they admit it?"*

Easy enough until a little rain shuts beaches down . . .

Did it mean nothing to you Animal that turns this
Planet to a smokey rock?
Back among your quarrels
How can I remind you of your gentleness?

> Jeans are washed
> Shells all lost or broken
> Driftwood sits in shadow boxes on a tracthouse wall

Like swallows you were, gathering
Like people I wish for . . .

> cannot even tell this to that fisherman

5.

3 of us in a boat the size of a bathtub   .   pitching in
slow waves   .   fish poles over the side   .   oars

We rounded a point of rock and entered a small cove

Below us:
             fronds of kelp
             fish
             crustaceans
             eels
Then us
             then rocks at the cliff's base
             starfish
             (hundreds of them sunning themselves)
             final starfish on the highest rock then
Cliff
             4 feet up the cliff a flower
             grass
             further up more grass
             grass over the cliff's edge
             branch of pine then
Far up the sky

             a hawk

Clutching to our chip we are jittering in a spectrum
Hung in the film of this narrow band
Green
             to our eyes only

6.

On a trail not far from here
Walking in meditation
We entered a dark grove
And I lost all separation in step with the
Eucalyptus as the trail walked back beneath me

Does it need to be that dark or is
Darkness only its occasion
Finding it by ourselves knowing
Of course
Somebody else was there before . . .

I like playing that game
Standing on a high rock looking way out over it all:

"I think I'll call it the Pacific"

Wind water
Wave rock
Sea sand

(there is no separation)

Wind that wets my lips is salt
Sea breaking within me balanced as the
Sea that floods these rocks. Rock
Returning to the sea, easily, as
Sea once rose from it. It
Is a sea rock

(easily)

I am
Rocked by the sea

TWO LIKE VILLANELLES

They're tearing down all the Victorian Mansions and
building Freeways in Portland Oregon & everywhere

"and the rough places
shall be plane"

In a landscape of ruined buildings,
on a small rock wheeling about the heavens and
        comin' on green to crack sidewalks,
you looked so beautiful picking blackberries
        all the long summer afternoon.

The berries!
Berries made fountains of fruit and thorn on
        rubble, iron fence and gate, on
basement steps to basement now just
berry-pit.

And you!
You looked so beautiful picking blackberries,
        long black hair in the summer sun, black eyes
glancing up to where I stood

In a landscape of ruined buildings,
on a small green rock

        wheeling about the heavens

For all the Wet Green Girls

I found myself, green girls, in a month like May,
in a green green garden at the break of day

all around me gray rain beat
and the cage that I am was an empty zoo

in a garden, girls, at a break like May
in the first wet light of the sun

when, from a rock in the arbor lept
a sleeping cat, through

gray green cages of deserted zoo
where I found myself on a breaking day

as bright rain beat upon the garden stone
where the lept cat left his belly print

alone, young girls, when my head unbent
in a green green garden at the break of day

and I saw what came
and I watched what went

Green Girls

NOTES FROM A PIONEER ON A SPECK IN SPACE

Few things that grow here poison us.
Most of the animals are small.
Those big enough to kill us do it in a way
Easy to understand, easy to defend against.
The air, here, is just what the blood needs.
We don't use helmets or special suits.

The Star, here, doesn't burn you if you
Stay outside as much as you should.
The worst of our winters is bearable.
Water, both salt and sweet, is everywhere.
The things that live in it are easily gathered.
Mostly, you can eat them raw with safety and pleasure.

Yesterday my wife and I brought back
Shells, driftwood, stones, and other curiosities
Found on the beach of the immense
Fresh-water Sea we live by.
She was all excited by a slender white stone which:
"Exactly fits the hand!"

I couldn't share her wonder;
Here, almost everything does.

HERMIT POEMS

(For Lloyd Reynolds)

PREFACE TO HERMIT POEMS, THE BATH

At last it is raining, the first sign of spring.
The Blue Jay gets all wet.

Frost-flowers, tiny bright and dry like
inch high crystal trees or sparkling silver mold,
acres of them, on heaps of placer boulders all around me,
are finally washing away. They were beautiful.
And the big trees rising, dark, behind them.

This canyon is so steep we didn't get sun since late November,
my "CC" shack and I. Obsolete. The two of us.
He for his de-funct agency.
I for this useless Art?

> *"Oughtta come by more often, Lewie,*
> *you get shack simple."*

big winter boom of the river
crunch of boots on the icy trail to it

kerosene lantern even in the daytime   golden light

inside

I think I'll bathe in
Spring-rain tin-roof clatter of it
all begins to melt away.
The bath a ritual here, the way it used to be.

> *Vat & Cauldron*
> *Kettle Pot & Tub*
> *Stoke the Stove till Cherry*

Naked, he clambers over boulders to his spring.
He dips two buckets full and scampers back.
Filling the many vessels on his stove, he starts
to rave.

I hear Incantations!
I hear voices of the Wise Old Men and
songs of the Addled Girls!

Moss! Astonishing green!
All that time the rocks were, even.

Hopping on it, wet, that Crested Blue!

Robin bedraggled.   Warm rain finally.   Spring.

[NOT YET 40, MY BEARD IS ALREADY WHITE.]

Not yet 40, my beard is already white.
Not yet awake, my eyes are puffy and red,
          like a child who has cried too much.

What is more disagreeable
than last night's wine?

I'll shave.
I'll stick my head in the cold spring and
look around at the pebbles.
Maybe I can eat a can of peaches.

Then I can finish the rest of the wine,
write poems till I'm drunk again,
and when the afternoon breeze comes up

I'll sleep until I see the moon
and the dark trees
and the nibbling deer

and hear
the quarreling coons

[I KNOW A MAN'S SUPPOSED TO HAVE HIS HAIR CUT SHORT]

I know a man's supposed to have his hair cut short,
but I have beautiful hair.
I like to let it grow into a long bronze mane.

In my boots. In my blue wool shirt.
With my rifle slung over my shoulder
among huge boulders in the dark ravine,

I'm the ghost roan stallion.
Leif Ericson.
The beautiful Golden Girl!

In summer I usually cut it all off.
I do it myself, with scissors and a
little Jim Beam.

How disappointed everybody is.

Months and months go by before they can
worry about my hairdo

and the breeze
is so cool

[APPARENTLY WASPS]

Apparently wasps
work all their only summer at the nest,
so that new wasps work
all their only summer at the nest,
et cetera.

All my lizards lost their tails, mating.
Six green snakes ate all my frogs.
Butterflies do very odd things with their tongues.

There seems to be no escaping it.
I planted nine tomato plants and water them.
I replaced my rotten stoop with a
clean Fir block.

Twelve new poems in less than a week!

[I BURN UP THE DEER IN MY BODY.]

I burn up the deer in my body.
I burn up the tree in my stove.

I seldom let a carrot go to seed, and I
grind up every kind of grain.

How can I be and never be an
inconvenience to others, here,

where only the Vulture is absolutely pure

and in the Chicago River
are carp?

Step out onto the Planet.
Draw a circle a hundred feet round.

Inside the circle are
300 things nobody understands, and, maybe
nobody's ever really seen.

How many can you find?

[THE EMPRESS HERSELF SERVED TEA TO SU TUNG-PO]

The Empress herself served tea to Su Tung-po,
and ordered him escorted home by
Ladies of the Palace, with torches.

I forgot my flashlight.
Drunk, I'll never get across this
rickety bridge.

Even the Lady in the Sky abandons me.

[WHENEVER I MAKE A NEW POEM,]

Whenever I make a new poem,
the old ones sound like gibberish.
How can they ever make sense in a book?

Let them say:
"He seems to have lived in the mountains.
He traveled now and then.
When he appeared in cities,
he was almost always drunk.

"Most of his poems are lost.
Many of those we have were found in
letters to his friends.

"He had a very large number of friends."

[THE IMAGE, AS IN A HEXAGRAM:]

The image, as in a Hexagram:

The hermit locks his door against the blizzard.
He keeps the cabin warm.

All winter long he sorts out all he has.
What was well started shall be finished.
What was not, should be thrown away.

In spring he emerges with one garment
and a single book.

The cabin is very clean.

Except for that, you'd never guess
anyone lived there.

[I SAW MYSELF]

I saw myself
a ring of bone
in the clear stream
of all of it

and vowed,
always to be open to it
that all of it
might flow through

and then heard
"ring of bone" where
ring is what a

bell does

THE WAY BACK

HE PREPARES TO TAKE LEAVE OF HIS HUT

And They, The Blessed Ones, said to him,
"Beautiful trip, Avalokiteshvara.
You never have to go back there again."

And he said, "Thank you very much, but I think I will.
Those people need all the help they can get."

      Not that I'm on the
      Other Side of the River, you understand,
      except literally.

      To get to the shack I found, you have to
      cross a rickety bridge of splintered boards, of
      cables, rusty, small, not really
      tied anymore to Alder trees.

      And a Raccoon takes a shit on it,
      almost every day, right where I have to
      step to get across.

      And should I wonder if it's
      fear, malevolence, or chance that
      makes him do this thing to me,

      when nothing's really stained by it,
      and yesterday a Butterfly sat down on it

              Butterfly on a Coon Turd
              A wet, blue, Jay

And even that is just a
pretty imitation of a
state of Mind I don't possess

or even seek, right now, or
wait for anymore.

"Why should it be so hard to give up
seeking something you know you can't possess?"

"Who ever said it was easy?"

HE ASKS FOR GUIDANCE

Avalokiteshvara, Buddha of Compassion, Original
Bodhisattva, Who spoke the Prajnaparamita Sutra
of the heart,

Kannon in Japan, Kuan-Yin in China, Chenrezig in
Tibet, No God, but guide, O
Countless thousands of returning men and women
of every place and time,

as Virgil for Dante, through Dante's Hell,

please guide me through Samsara.

HE WRITES TO THE DONOR OF HIS BOWL

November 25, 1962

Albert,

The last thing I ate in the beautiful bowl you made & gave me
was a Salmon Chippino (perhaps misspelled & not in my
Webster's dictionary)

Old Bill Allen & I went out for mushrooms, but it's been too long
since rain & the mushrooms are wormy or rotten or both

& while I went to the car for a pull on the wine-jug Bill got all
excited pointing at the creek & motioning me downstream
("you pitch, I'll catch" I always say to the old men on this river
who can't very well scramble across wet rocks anymore, though
they shoot very straight)

& he shot this salmon with his 30-30 & I got wet to the knees
catching it as it washed downstream (not being able to pick
my spot)

What he didn't know is, salmon stay nicely in that pool so there
isn't any hurry, but he hurried, & I barely got the cap back on
the bottle & splashed in the creek & grabbed it (both hands just
above the tail & lift — that way they seem unable to move, as I
learned on commercial fishing boats)

You boil potatoes, celery, onions & garlic in a little water & when
they are almost done you dump in chunks of Salmon (or whatever
fish or crabs) A little later add a can of stewed tomatoes.

It was good fish stew made better by the bowl you made.

Thank you,

New

HE THANKS HIS WOODPILE

The wood of the madrone burns with a flame at once
lavender and mossy green, a color you sometimes see in a sari.

Oak burns with a peppery smell.

For a really hot fire, use bark.
You can crack your stove with bark.

All winter long I make wood stews:

Poem to stove to woodpile to stove to
typewriter.   woodpile.   stove.

and can't stop peeking at it!
can't stop opening up the door!
can't stop giggling at it

"Shack Simple"

crazy as Han Shan as
Wittgenstein in his German hut, as
all the others ever were and are

Ancient Order of the Fire Gigglers

who walked away from it, finally,
kicked the habit, finally, of Self, of
man-hooked Man

(which is not, at last, estrangement)

A SONG TO HIS SECRET FARM

for Robert Creeley

Grow, little plant!
Show those who waste my time and thee
How good it is to be
As any weed.

—Jungle Thing!

Fear not though deer shall
Surely clip thy life, be
Stoical,
Like I

It was for Love you came so far
To germinate

And die!

FAREWELL TO HIS BIRDS AND ANIMALS

Richer than the richest Falconer,
I hold my hawks and canyons light as time.

"Just happening along," as they say

> for a flutter
> for a wing-fold terrifying
> drop

(a small explosion on the ground!)

> dust & feathers
> rodent squeek

(his dinner's dangling down!)

HE PRAISES HIS CANYONS & PEAKS

Driving out to Callahan, you get the setting for it all:

    Cloud-shrouded gorges!
    Foggy trees!

    I can't see the ridges anymore!
    River?

Big Sung landscape scroll a

mile high and

    longer than I'll ever know!

HE GREETS, AGAIN, THE OPEN ROAD

Shut the shack door,
packed the car, and
drove to San Francisco
400 miles through valleys of larks —

    the hills that year so green a
    sheen of gold cast over them,
    as if the eye just couldn't
    stand such green

        and not a single Poppy!
        State Flower
        spookily gone

But I don't care in my Survival Car when
O, my Lady loves to ride with me!

        hot whiskey
        long concrete
        back seat
        rifle food & sleeping bag

Motionless, finally, finally just
drifting along on concrete belt going
70-miles-an-hour underneath my car
Still, except for the swing of the steering wheel, and
She!
my Lady loves to sing to me!

        anarchist lectures 5 hours long,
        songs all winter wrong set right

(and won't even let me stop to scribble them down)

Hot
Whiskey

Long concrete

Big Chevvy Engine 6-Ply Song how

Shrineless, I

pilgrim

        through the world

HE FINALLY REACHES THE CITY

Woke up sick and old, in somebody else's bed

"somewhere in the Universe"

to a glass of orange juice, a note

(how she had to go to work and what
the phone and when,

Gloria   X X X)

Celsus?   Day?   O!

Warm glass of water in the bathroom strange towels
bottles, goo. Ubiquitous
crazy razor hopeless lady-blades

*"I don't know who you are, but
I'm going to shave you anyway."*

•

Diet pills in the medicine chest!

(terrible vision of hyped-up ladies
much too skinny anyway Amphetamine
suburb babble!

Nowhere? Nowhere, anymore, that
fat & lovely Mother-Flesh to
lay our heads upon

"There there, Lewie," nursely.
almost unconcerned

as if her flesh were there
to give a rest to
new flesh, thinner,
growing, and
sometimes scared . . .

kids fidgety in the suburbs

the Mothers "Handsome")

Check the milligrams, take the necessary dose
Forward! Into Day!

Damp, towel about my loins,
back to scented room, to
orange juice, to
Miracle!
           (2 full inches left of Vodka)

       •

Is this, then, the
Mystical Return? The
Man come back?

        The Red Monk used to say:

        "Find yourself at some ridiculous task,
        say, urinating in the hostess's flower bed,
        the party raging on, above,

        and imagine all your life, and past lives,
        till you see them vividly. Then,

        shaking off the dew, say out loud:

        So,
        It has all come to this?

       •

On with the groovey boots.
On with essential shades against the glare

    (remembering Lamantia's poem

        Blue Grace
        behind dark glasses

        Steps out of a
        hundred white cars

        all over town . . .)

How clean it looked, that walked out through the door!

    Ah City!
        I would tell you how it was to
    stalk your streets!

    So young!   *Anonymous!*

HE LOCATES THE LIVE MUSEUM

For Kirby Doyle,
remembering his house in
Larkspur

Finally there's no room for it all. Masterpieces lean face
against the wall, and the trail on up to it is littered with sculpture.
Mushrooms grow in a Theater for Artaud.

And you can't put your hand down, even accidentally,
without it coming back with a treasure in it—some flake off
the Planet, or a spooky little box.

When you open the door, it's funky-beaded, feathered, and
white.

Wine! How beautiful! We were almost out of wine!

Has anybody ever said, out loud, that our job is to give ourselves
away? That now and then we must have rest from that work?
That this is the resting place?

The Mountain Man returns. The soldier returns. The shy
inhabiter of rooms, returns. The husband returns. The frightened
girl. The boy who cannot tell, just yet, how right he is.

Embracing. Everyone embracing.

Where we show us what we made in solitude. Where we
tell us everything we know.

Where we catch our breath, and weep.

We sit on each others laps and look into our eyes, where
the dancer who is actually a fawn plays flute and the girls, who
are all of them sisters, sing and sew.

We are "drowsed," as Keats used to say, "By the fumes of
poppies."

It's hard to understand Collectors. Impossible to make them see it's made and made and made and can't be kept. I drink to them. I smoke to them. I pity them. I've given up. I cannot ever share my bliss.

Coffee in a shakey cup.

Crash of last night's bottles in the garbage pit.

Bedding aired and put away the
girls, now, plaiting each other's hair and
painting on their eyes, and

Look, Lewie,

Here comes another one!

all of us sharing Wonder as it breaks again across our hills

the Sun

HE BEGINS TO RECOUNT HIS ADVENTURES

I can't remember seeing it any other way but whole, a big round rock wheeling about the heavens and comin' on green to crack sidewalks, gentle and undemanding, as if I saw it first, approaching it from somewhere else.

Everything about it always seemed right. The roundness is right. The way it spins.

I used to wonder why you couldn't break every speed record just by going straight up and somehow hang up there awhile, while the world spun around beneath you.

Suppose you dug a tunnel all the way to China and then jumped into the hole. You'd fall down through the center, and then fall up — almost to the other side. Then you'd fall back down again, up again, down again, each time losing a little distance, till finally you'd be hanging there, exactly in the middle — the only place in the world where every way is up.

Somebody said it's way too hot in there and nobody could possibly do it. Others thought I'd shoot out way up over China and then fall back and miss the hole ('cause the world would turn a little in the meantime) and just end up killing my damn fool self.

But I liked the part at the very end, when you're falling only 50 feet or so, through and back and through again, like a very slow kind of floating quiver or something.

You could bounce on it, later, or even walk around on it (in it, through it). You keep going *through* it all the time. Like those dolls with weighted bottoms only you don't ever have a table top to end up right side up on. A weird bouncy sort of spin thing you couldn't ever get out of. You could try, but you'd never make it: 3,959 miles straight up in all directions.

All the colors are right. We say it's mostly green and blue, but other animals see it differently than that and when you get up high enough it all gets black, so maybe it's just our eyes that make the colors right.

The balance of land and water is right — a very good thing in a spinning ball. If too much weight were on one side it'd shake itself to pieces, or get into some wacky eccentric extra orbit kind thing — worse and worse till finally it all breaks loose from the Sun's pull and wings on out into nowhere, crashing into planets and suns and generally causing all kinds of unimaginable hassles and disasters.

Not only is the land and water balanced right, the shapes are very beautiful. The two big land-shapes are strikingly similar, for example, and right. They both have narrow places near the middle — the right place to be narrow.

Everything is right, clear down to the smallest parts of it. I know a beach that's made up entirely of little round stones the size of a pea or smaller. All smooth and round little pieces of jade, jasper, agate, moonstones, glass from broken bottles, shells, tiny pieces of wood — and you get so hung up in a few square yards you just can't stop collecting and hunting and looking into it and suddenly there's an unbelievably tiny little pure white claw of a crab and *on that* is something even smaller, crawling!

Even smaller than that, it's right. You can spend your whole life looking through microscopes at subworlds living off further subworlds, just as surely as looking through a telescope at light years and light years of worlds so far away they aren't even there anymore — nothing's there except this little blip of light that finally travelled far enough to hit your human eyeball and live, thereby. The whole thing finally coming together as Rexroth said: . . . "like looking at a drop of ink and suddenly finding you're looking at the Milky Way."

Or John Muir waking in a Sierra meadow, in spring, and finding, inches from his waking eye, a wildflower he, and nobody else, had ever seen. Rising, he found himself in a field of delicate color so complicated he spent the whole day in only ten square feet of it, classifying and drawing pictures of hundreds of little plants for the first time in the world.

An average of a ton of insects for every acre of a field like that. Deer-hoof crushing a flower. Rodents at the roots of it. Birds diving and pecking at it. Big trees crowding it out with their shade. Mushrooms in the warm fall rains.

Ridges rising into mountains and air too thin and not much dirt for it. Shy little Coneys nibbling at tiny moss. Snow and Glaciers and the peaks at last.

Eternal snow where no matter how far up it is you can bet your life some man, sometime, stood, and looked, and wept again for wonder of this Human eye!

HE EXPLAINS IT ANOTHER WAY

•

At times we're almost able to see it was once all

Light, and wants to get back to it.

Not brilliant, swift, or huge, since Light

is the measure, and we are

Flake off of All-Measure

Cinder cast down from Sun

(explaining every "fall" and why we yearn so?)

Harnessed jelly of the Stars!

•

DIN POEM

Tizuvthee, Old Soapy, land where Thoreau sat and Whitman
walked, despised of all nations, Strontium, alone

Tizuvthee

Fucked L.A. starlet of tiny dream untrue even to your
 tiny dream intolerable up-tight dirty noise New
 York, rusty muscle Chicago, hopeless Cleveland
 Akron Visalia alcoholic San Francisco suicide

Tizuvthee, I sing

SUPERMARKET SONG

Super Anahist cough syrup tastes as good as the syrup they put
 on ice cream.
Super Anahist cough syrup tastes as good as the syrup they put
 on ice cream.
Super Anahist cough syrup tastes as good as the syrup they put
 on ice cream.

        Let's take out the car and park it
        at the big new super market
        and go on inside and see
        what they got for you and me.

        Look at all the brand names!
        Aren't they really grand names!
        Continental Can Corporation of America
        has arranged that to be!

        Pepsi Cola, Coca-Cola,
        Rice Crispies & Del Monte
        Best Foods! Best Foods! Best Foods!

Everything is wrapped in plastic.
Everything begins to look like it came from L.A.
and they/deal out the pineapple Dole/
to better enable you to meet your role

as customer
of the big new super market
where we take our car and we park it,

and bread will never rot
and you've got to

Save the stamps!
Save the stamps!

Save the stamps
it's fun.

Hi Man, what's happening. See you people later.
Hi Man, what's happening. See you people later.
Hi Man, what's happening. See you people later.

            Lowering the butterfat
            to meet marketing requirements
            actually increases the
            percentage of Calcium,
            Potassium, Phosphorous,
            and other food elements

You could make this marriage work if you'd only try!

I am in Personnel.

Anti-personnel bomb. Exceptional Children. Homogenized.
Over-kill. Hydrogenated. Apostolic Faith. Pentecostal.

He died for our sins.

Pentecostal holy-mission. United Brotherhood of the Sons
of Father Baptism Apostolic. Virgin Mother house of
Grace the holy ghost immersion. Sanctuary redemption.
Death. Devil finds work for idle excommunicate. Confess
thy total pentecostal immersion, my son.

I pledge allegiance.

You never say you love me anymore.

NEVER. NEVER PUT THE GOD-DAMN CAMERA IN THE
GLOVE COMPARTMENT. I TOLD YOU AND TOLD YOU TO
NEVER PUT THE GOD-DAMN CAMERA IN THE GLOVE
COMPARTMENT. SO WHAT DO YOU DO? YOU PUT THE
GOD-DAMN CAMERA IN THE GLOVE COMPARTMENT.
AND IT'S STOLEN! SEE?

Nigger.
Nigger town.

Nigger car. Nigger suit. Gypsy.

Nigger gypsy poet wop. Jew.

Spic.

Nigger gypsy poet wop beatnic. Spic wop. Wop wop.

Jew nigger beatnic poet wop spic commie. Beat commie.
Poet commie. Faggot wop. Nigger.

Nigger house. Nigger fence. Nigger poet beatnic wop.

Wop wop. Dope fiend.

Dope fiend nigger. Yellah nigger. Nigger lovin' beatnic
wop. Nigger.

Ashtray nigger. Billboard nigger. Nigger wall nigger
suit nigger shoes nigger.

Nigger nigger.

Sunset.

Flower.

Nigger flower

The Christmas message carries a great and wondrous hope.
This hope, advanced with courage and determination, is a
very present help to you and to your doctors and nurses.
As they assist you in your effort for full recovery to
health, you can count upon the continuing gratitude and
concern of your fellow Americans.

Dwight D. Eisenhower

If I told you once,
I told you a thousand times

All right fella!

Where's your I.D.?

How long you lived at that address?

Get in the car.

"I don't know what's the matter honey, I'm not always this
way."

"Oh baby, that's all right, the sex thing is only a part
of it."

"Yeah but I want you so bad and the damned thing . . ."

"Ahh, don't worry about it, please, the sex thing . . ."

"I'm perfectly all right and then I try to roll on top
and the god damn thing . . ."

"Shhh. Shhh. Don't. I mean it, really, it's all right.
Really baby. The sex thing's only a little part of it and . . ."

Here kitty kitty. Here kitty kitty kitty. Where's that
damn cat anyway. Kitty? Here kitty kitty. Here you
god damn kitty kitty . . .

Apostolic Faith Mission Love in Christ of God Salvation
gave his life for YOU in virgin house of love lady in
Christ BEHOLDEN and KNOW, *Believe* on his words better to
avoid the bait of sin than STRUGGLE on the hook, beholden,
hope. Nameless name IMMACULATE yearning for him
DAUGHTERS of sin beholden and NOT ASKED before his
THRONE!

You've been late four times this month.

Jiveassmuthafucka, Javassmuthafucka

Jive.   Ass.   Mother.   Fucker.

Chickens can't lay eggs unless there's a rooster around
can they?

What's that girl doing down the hall, anyway?

Where you workin' fella?   Get in the car.

Let's get him fixed. They're much nicer pets if you get 'em
fixed.

Do you still feel bad?

I am on top of the Empire State Building leaning on the
railing which I have carefully examined to see if it's
strongly made. The sound of it comes all that way, up,
to me. A hum. Thousands of ventilators far away. Now
and then I hear an improbable clank. The air, even up
here, is warmed by it.

To the north a large green rectangle, Central Park, lies
flat, clean-edged, indented. A skin has been pulled off,
a bandage removed, and a small section of the Planet has
been allowed to grow.

I think, "They have chosen to do this in order to save
their lives." And then I think, "It is not really a section
of the Planet, it is a perfect imitation of a section of the Planet
(remembering the zoo). It is how they think it might look."
I am struck by their wisdom.   Moved.

The elevator is not too crowded. We are all silent and
perfectly behaved, except a little girl who is whispering
something to her mother. Her mother holds her hand and
bends down to listen. The little girl giggles. Hunching
her shoulders and screwing up her face. She has told her
mother something outrageous.

In the lobby are people who are really doing it, not like us,
just looking around. They wear the current costume and read
the office directories beside the banks and banks of
elevators. I realize there are offices in the Empire State
Building! It is not just a tower to look from!

It all starts coming in, on the street. Each one is going
somewhere, thinking. Many are moving their lips, talking
to themselves. In 2 blocks I am walking as fast as they
are. We all agree to wait when the light turns red.

In the subway it is more intense. Something about being
under the ground? It is horrifying to let it all come in,
in the subway.

A small Jew with crazed eyes and a little bent old body is
carrying a shopping bag and is wearing two brown vests. He
has, for a walking stick, a length of curtain rod, solid brass.
He avoids a post and doesn't look into the large trash-basket.
His lips are moving.

A gust of dirty air hits me as I rise out of it at the 7th Ave.
subway exit. I am relieved, perhaps because the buildings
are lower, the street wider, the intersection a jumble of
crazy angles?

The white walls of an apartment generously lent by a girl
I hardly know. She moved up to the Bronx, to her mother's,
just to give us a place to stay. I lock the doors and think
how perfect an apartment it is.

The top of the brandy bottle is correctly designed. I don't
have to fuss with a difficult plastic seal. All I have to do is
twist it off.

Outside, a ventilator randomly clanks . . . . .

•

Years ago, somewhere inconceivably else, I could have been
given a strange assignment.

He was a short man, gray haired but mostly bald. He explained
the thing to me in a homey kind of office.

"I can fix you up to be, actually *be,* a Native of a World!"
he said. "You won't be *like* them, you will *be* one of them.
Think the way they do, see as they see etc. *with exactly
their physical and mental equipment.* You can see, of course,
what this means! It means your data, for the first time, will
be absolutely accurate. You will, in every sense, *know*
what it is to be one."

I have forgotten all he said about the reports I'd have to make
on my return, but I can almost remember the taste of the
potion I got. Brassy, but not too bad.

And what is happening during moments like that on the Empire State building is simply that the potion's effect is flickering out. There are moments of wakefulness, and it all starts coming in.

You see in on the faces of the others. They are all more or less drugged. Many are as straight or straighter than you are, but are pretending not to be. As you are pretending not to be.

It is then, while watching the ones who are actually doing it (not like us, just looking around), that you realize there are *only* people more or less drugged into this vast, insane, assignment.

There are no natives!

I pledge allegiance to the Pentecostal Brotherhood of the Faith in. I never felt worse. Do you still feel bad? How long have you lived at that address? Get in the car.

I've never been so ashamed in my life.

You don't know how much better I feel. It's like having some beautiful thing protecting you all the time. A soft and lovely power that's devoted only to good. Get in the car.

"It's called Conation and Affect."

Exceptional Children. Anti-Personnel Bomb. Top Secret.

"What kind of books does he read?"

I told you a thousand times.

It is better not to marry but it is better to marry than to burn. Water seeks its own level.

You've been late four times this month.

You could make this marriage work if you'd only try.

Adieu, adieu

Soleil cou coupé

Meadowlark

Dove

COURSES

No Credit No Blame No Balm

COURSE COLLEGE CREDO

We refuse the right to serve anybody.

GEOGRAPHY

The Far East is west of us,
nearer by far
than the Near East,
and mysteriouser.

Is the Middle East
really the Middle West?

And there aren't 7 continents,
there are 6—

Europe and Asia are
stuck together

in the middle.

HISTORY

Every 30 years or so, Elders arm Children
with expensive weapons and send them away
to kill other children similarly armed.

Some do not return. Some return
maimed or terrified into madness.
Many come back brutal.

Nothing else changes.

Mr. Krupp got the whole works back
by producing a single document

from his briefcase.

AESTHETICS

Not very many can do it really well.

Nobody knows why.

MATH

One and one makes two. There is a
two which is one,
at last. One alone is lonely.

Three is possible.
There are plenty of holes for everybody.

Four is nearly impossible.
Try it.

A great mathematician
(and this is a true story),
while waiting in a brothel and
looking at dirty pictures,

suddenly got the vision of
all the combinations of all the
plugs and holes of Nine.

Excited, he ran home and invented our
theorems of combinations and permutations.

That day, he didn't get laid.

THEOLOGY

The True Rebel never advertises it,
He prefers His joy to Missionary Work.

Church is Bureaucracy,
no more interesting than any Post Office.

Religion is Revelation:
all the Wonder of all the Planets striking
all your Only Mind.

Guard the Mysteries!
Constantly reveal Them!

PSYCHOLOGY

The trouble is
most people spend their lives living it

down.

BOTANY

Consider the Passion Flower:

Who'd ever think a plant would go to
so much trouble

just to get fucked
by a Bee.

PHILOSOPHY

Never ask Why What,
Always ask What's What.
Observe, connect, and do.

The great Winemaster is almost a
magician to the bulk of his Tribe,
to his Peers he is only accurate.

"He knows the Grape so well," they say,

"He turned into a Vine."

THE BASIC CON

Those who can't find anything to live for,
always invent something to die for.

Then they want the rest of us to
die for it, too.

These, and an elite army of thousands,
who do nobody any good at all, but do
great harm to some,
have always collected vast sums from all.

Finally, all this machinery
tries to kill us,

because we won't die for it, too.

[POSTGRADUATE COURSES]

LAW

He who chooses for the chicken
gives bounty for the Bob-Cat

COMPORTMENT

Think Jew
Dance nigger
Dress and drive Oakie

COURSE COLLEGE GRADUATION ADDRESS

(1) Freak out.
(2) Come back.
(3) Bandage the wounded and feed
however many you can.
(4) Never cheat.

COURSE COLLEGE OATH

All persecutors
Shall be violated!

THE SONG MT. TAMALPAIS SINGS

This is the last place. There is nowhere else to go.

       Human movements,
           but for a few,
       are Westerly.
       Man follows the Sun.

This is the last place. There is nowhere else to go.

       Or follows what he thinks to be the
       movement of the Sun.
       It is hard to feel it, as a rider,
       on a spinning ball.

This is the last place. There is nowhere else to go.

       Centuries and hordes of us,
       from every quarter of the earth,
       now piling up,
       and each wave going back
       to get some more.

This is the last place. There is nowhere else to go.

       "My face is the map of the Steppes,"
       she said, on this mountain, looking West.

       My blood set singing by it,
       to the old tunes,
       Irish, still,
       among these Oaks.

This is the last place.   There is nowhere else to go.

This is why
once again we celebrate
the great Spring Tides.

Beaches are strewn again with Jasper,
Agate, and Jade.
The Mussel-rock stands clear.

This is the last place.   There is nowhere else to go.

This is why
once again we celebrate the
Headland's huge, cairn-studded, fall
into the Sea.

This is the last place.   There is nowhere else to go.

For we have walked the jeweled beaches
at the feet of the final cliffs
of all Man's wanderings.

This is the last place.
There is nowhere else we need to go.

OLEMA SATORI

for Peter Coyote

Walking from the gate to the farmhouse,

Buzzards wheeling close as 20-feet,
to the West a ridge of
Redwoods, Fir, that
goofey Pt. Reyes pine,

walking on a dirt farm road,

small birds darting from the grass,
cows, burnt hills,
tongue of the Pacific,
ridge and the Last Ocean,
my boots,
walking,

"This is all you get,"
Olema said.

And I said, "That's
twice as much as I could ever hope for."

And Peter said,

"You can have the whole thing,
with fur covered pillows,

at the same price."

SAUSALITO TRASH PRAYER

Sausalito,
> *Little Willow,*
Perfect Beach by the last Bay in the world,
> *None more beautiful,*

Today we kneel at thy feet
> *And curse the men who have misused you.*

PRAYER TO A MOUNTAIN SPRING

> *Gentle Goddess,*

> *Who never asks for anything at all,*
> *and gives us everything we have,*

> *thank you for this sweet water,*

> *and your fragrance.*

THE RIDDLE OF HANDS

In every culture, in every place and time, there has always been a religion, and in every one of these religions there has always been the gesture of hands clasped together, as Christians do to pray, in order to signify something important.

Why is this?

(There is only one right answer to this riddle)

COMMENTARY BY THE RED MONK

The gesture has but one source. Who would think to pick his nose, or cross his eyes, at such a moment?
The man who claims to feel power between his hands is lost in forms and ideas. The man who clasps his hands and waits will never see the light.

THE RIDDLE OF BOWING

In every culture, in every place and time, there has always been a religion, and in every one of these religions there has always been the gesture of bowing so fully that the forehead strikes the ground.

Why is this?

(There is only one right answer to this riddle)

COMMENTARY BY THE RED MONK

Sooner or later the gesture is necessary no matter which way you go. Suzuki bows with so much confidence we all feel bold.

THE RIDER RIDDLE

If you spend as much time on the Mountain as you should, She will always give you a Sentient Being to ride: animal, plant, insect, reptile, or any of the Numberless Forms.

What do *you* ride?

(There is one right answer for every person, and only that person can really know what it is)

COMMENTARY BY THE RED MONK

Manjusri rode a tiger. One, just as fierce as he, rode a mouse. There is no one who can tell you what the answer is. The Mountain will show you.

REDWOOD HAIKU

Orange, the brilliant slug—
Nibbling at the leaves of
Trillium

DIFFICULTY ALONG THE WAY

Seeking Perfect Total Enlightenment
is looking for a flashlight
when all you need the flashlight for
is to find your flashlight

I SOMETIMES TALK TO
KEROUAC WHEN I DRIVE

Jack?

Yesterday I thought of something
I never had a chance to tell you
and now I don't know what it was

Remember?

83

SPRINGTIME IN THE ROCKIES, LICHEN

All these years I overlooked them in the
racket of the rest, this
symbiotic splash of plant and fungus feeding
on rock, on sun, a little moisture, air —
tiny acid-factories dissolving
salt from living rocks and
eating them.

Here they are, blooming!
Trail rock, talus and scree, all dusted with it:
rust, ivory, brilliant yellow-green, and
cliffs like murals!
Huge panels streaked and patched, quietly
with shooting-stars and lupine at the base.

Closer, with the glass, a city of cups!
Clumps of mushrooms and where do the
plants begin? Why are they doing this?
In this big sky and all around me peaks &
the melting glaciers, why am I made to
kneel and peer at Tiny?

These are the stamps on the final envelope.

How can the poisons reach them?
In such thin air, how can they care for the
loss of a million breaths?
What, possibley, could make their ground more bare?

Let it all die.

The hushed globe will wait and wait for
what is now so small and slow to
open it again.

As now, indeed, it opens it again, this
scentless velvet,
crumbler-of-the-rocks,

this Lichen!

WARNING OF TAMALPAIS

Let all quick-eyed, pride-full girls
take note of this

and every willing, head-strong boy
beware:

Nothing, in all the Universe, is more
sickening to see
than a good man, trying, and he

plagued by a bad woman!

SONG OF THE TURKEY BUZZARD

For Rock Scully
who heard it
the first
time

Praises, Tamalpais,
Perfect in Wisdom and Beauty,
She of the Wheeling Birds

I.

The rider riddle is easy to ask,
but the answer might surprise you.

How desperately I wanted Cougar
(I, Leo, etc.)
                brilliant proofs: terrain,
color, food, all
nonsense. All made up.

They were always there, the
laziest high-flyers, bronze-winged,
the silent ones

"A cunning man always laughs and smiles,
                even if he's desperately hungry,
while a good bird always flies like a vulture,
                even if it is starving."

(Milarepa sang)

Over and over again, that sign:

I hit one once, with a .22
heard the "flak" and a feather flew off, he
flapped his wings just once and
went on sailing. Bronze

(when seen from above)

as I have seen them, all day sitting
on a cliff so steep they
circled below me, in the up-draft
passed so close I could see his
eye.

Praises Tamalpais,
Perfect in Wisdom and Beauty,
She of the Wheeling Birds

Another time the vision was so clear another saw it, too.
Wet, a hatching bird, the shell of the egg streaked with dry scum,
exhausted, wet, too weak to move the shriveled wings, fierce
sun-heat, sand. Twitching, as with elbows (we all have the same
parts). Beak open, neck stretched, gasping for air. O how we
want to live!

"Poor little bird," she said, "he'll never make it."

Praises, Tamalpais,
Perfect in Wisdom & Beauty,
She of the Wheeling Birds

Even so, I didn't get it for a long long while. It finally came
in a trance, a coma, half in sleep and half in fever-mind. A Turkey
Buzzard, wounded, found by a rock on the mountain. He wanted
to die alone. I had never seen one, wild, so close. When I reached
out, he sidled away, head drooping, as dizzy as I was. I put my
hands on his wing-shoulders and lifted him. He tried, feebly, to
tear at my hands with his beak. He tore my flesh too slightly to
make any difference. Then he tried to heave his great wings. Weak
as he was, I could barely hold him.

A drunken veterinarian found a festering bullet in his side,
a .22 that slid between the great bronze scales his feathers were.
We removed it and cleansed the wound.

Finally he ate the rotten gophers I trapped and prepared for him. Even at first, he drank a lot of water. My dog seemed frightened of him.

They smell sweet
    meat is dry on their talons

The very opposite of
    death

bird of re-birth
    Buzzard

meat is rotten meat made
    sweet again and

lean, unkillable, wing-locked
    soarer till he's but a

speck in the highest sky
    infallible

eye finds Feast! on
    baked concrete

    free!

squashed rabbit ripened:
    our good cheese

(to keep the highways clean, and bother no Being)

II.

Praises Gentle Tamalpais
Perfect in Wisdom and Beauty of the
sweetest water
and the soaring birds

great seas at the feet of thy cliffs

Hear my last Will & Testament:

Among my friends there shall always be
one with proper instructions
for my continuance.

Let no one grieve.
I shall have used it all up
used up every bit of it.

What an extravagance!
What a relief!

On a marked rock, following his orders,
place my meat.

All care must be taken not to
frighten the natives of this
barbarous land, who
will not let us die, even,
as we wish.

With proper ceremony disembowel what I
no longer need, that it might more quickly
rot and tempt

my new form

NOT THE BRONZE CASKET BUT THE BRAZEN WING

SOARING FOREVER ABOVE THEE O PERFECT

O SWEETEST WATER O GLORIOUS

WHEELING

BIRD

INDEX OF TITLES AND FIRST LINES

Titles of poems are given in Italic type

GREY FOX PRESS BOOKS